# Unlocking the Secrets of Athletic Performance:

## *An Intro to Strength Training and Conditioning*

By

**Chuck S. Martinez**

# TABLE OF CONTENTS

# Introductions

John had been an athlete all his life, but as he got older, he noticed that he was losing his edge. He was getting slower, and weaker, and he was having a harder time competing. He knew he needed to do something to improve his performance, so he decided to look into the book Unlocking the Secrets of Athletic Performance: An Intro to Strength Training and Conditioning

John read up on the basics of strength training and conditioning and began to understand the importance of proper form and technique. He learned about the different types of exercises and how to safely perform them. He also learned about nutrition and how to fuel his body for peak performance.

With the help of a knowledgeable coach, John began to implement a rigorous strength training and conditioning program. He began to see results almost immediately as he felt stronger and faster than ever before. He was able to reach new heights in his performance, and he felt more confident in his abilities.

John continued to train and condition, and soon his performance was no longer a cause of concern. He was able to stay ahead of the competition with ease and even set a few personal bests. He was thrilled with the results he achieved and was glad that he had taken the time to learn about strength training and conditioning.

John now looks back on the decision he made to explore strength training and conditioning as one of the best decisions he ever made. He knows that it was a key factor in unlocking the secrets of athletic performance.

John now uses his newfound knowledge to help other athletes reach their goals and improve their performance. He is thankful that he was able to take the time to learn about strength training and conditioning, and he is proud of the results he achieved.

John continues to use strength training and conditioning as part of his athletic routine, and he looks forward to seeing the results it will bring in the future. With the help of strength training and conditioning, John was able to unlock the secrets of athletic performance.

Unlocking the Secrets of Athletic Performance: An Intro to Strength Training and Conditioning provides an introduction to the science and practice of improving athletic performance. This book provides an overview of the physiology of exercise and performance, principles of strength training, and exercise prescription and program design. The book covers the basics of anatomy and biomechanics, as well as the principles of sports nutrition and sports psychology. Additionally, the book reviews the latest research on the physiological and psychological effects of exercise and its impact on performance.

The book is written for athletes, coaches, and trainers who are interested in gaining a better understanding of how to design and implement an effective strength training and conditioning program. The authors provide detailed information on the body's response to exercise and the various components of an effective program, including warm-up and cool-down techniques, selection of exercises, periodization, and rest and recovery. The book also includes sample programs for various sports and fitness goals, such as developing power, strength, speed, and endurance.

Overall, this book provides an excellent introduction to the science and practice of strength training and conditioning. It is an invaluable resource for any athlete, coach, or trainer who is looking to maximize their performance and reach their goals.

Unlocking the Secrets of Athletic Performance: An Intro to Strength Training and Conditioning is an important resource for anyone interested in the science and practice of strength training and conditioning. It provides a comprehensive overview of the principles of strength training and exercise prescription, as well as the latest research on the physiological and psychological effects of exercise. This book is an invaluable resource for athletes, coaches, and trainers who are looking to maximize their performance and reach their goals.

# Chapter 1

## Basics of Athletic Performance

Athletic performance is the ability of an athlete to perform at the highest level of their sport. It is a combination of physical and mental skills, as well as the dedication and commitment of the athlete to continually strive to improve their performance. To become a successful athlete, one must have proper athletic training and conditioning, combined with a healthy diet and lifestyle.

Physical conditioning is the foundation of any successful athletic performance. An athlete must have a well-rounded physical condition to be successful. Proper warm-ups, stretching, strength training, and cardio training are all important components of physical conditioning. An athlete should also focus on flexibility, balance, coordination, and core stability. All of these components are necessary for an athlete to maximize their performance.

Mental conditioning is also an important part of athletic performance. Athlete needs to be able to control their emotions, stay focused, and make quick decisions when necessary. Developing a strong mental game can help an athlete to stay composed and confident during competition.

Nutrition is also an important factor in athletic performance. Eating a balanced diet and making sure to get the right number of macronutrients, vitamins, and minerals are essential for athletes. Proper hydration is also important, as dehydration can lead to fatigue and performance-related issues.

Finally, an athlete must commit to excellence to reach their peak performance. This includes having a positive attitude, setting goals, and having the discipline to follow through with them. It also requires having a good support system and belief in oneself. With the right combination of physical, mental, and nutrition, an athlete can reach their full potential and maximize their athletic performance.

In summary, athletic performance is a combination of physical, mental, and nutritional components. It is essential for athletes to have a well-rounded physical condition and mental game, as well as a healthy diet and lifestyle, to maximize their performance. With a commitment to excellence and the right support system, any athlete can reach their peak performance.

# Chapter 2

## Understanding Strength Training

Strength training is a type of physical exercise that is designed to build up muscles and improve overall strength. Athletes need to understand the basics of strength training so that they can effectively use it to improve their performance.

The most basic form of strength training involves lifting weights. By focusing on specific muscle groups and performing a variety of exercises, athletes can work on building muscle and improving strength. It is important to remember that each muscle group should be worked on separately and with different exercises. This will help ensure a balanced workout and avoid overworking any particular muscle group.

Another important factor to consider when strength training is the use of proper form. Proper form is essential for reducing the risk of injury and maximizing the benefits of exercise.

Proper form involves keeping the core and lower back engaged to support the weight, keeping the spine in a neutral position, and keeping the joints in alignment.

In addition to lifting weights, other types of strength-training exercises can be used to improve strength. These include bodyweight exercises such as squats and push-ups, plyometric exercises such as box jumps and burpees, and endurance exercises such as running and cycling.

Finally, athletes need to understand the importance of nutrition for strength training. Eating a balanced diet and getting enough protein, carbohydrates, and healthy fats are essential for building muscle and maintaining strength.

Understanding the basics of strength training is important for athletes who want to improve their performance. By focusing on proper form, different types of exercises, and proper nutrition, they can maximize their strength training and reach their goals.

Understanding strength training gives athletes the tools they need to make the most of their workouts and reach their goals.

It makes the training more effective and safer. It helps them target and build specific muscles, and it helps them understand the importance of nutrition and how to properly fuel their bodies. With the right knowledge and training, athletes can reach their strength-training goals and improve their performance.

In conclusion, understanding strength training is critical for athletes who want to improve their performance. It is important to know the basics of strength training, how to use proper form, the different types of exercises, and the importance of nutrition. With this knowledge, athletes can maximize their workouts and reach their strength-training goals.

# Chapter 3

## Developing a Strength Training Program

Developing a strength training program can be a great way to improve physical fitness, increase muscle mass, and increase overall health. Strength training can be tailored to individual needs, and should include exercises that target all major muscle groups.

Before beginning a strength training program, it's important to consult a doctor to ensure that you are healthy enough for exercise.

Once you have the green light from your doctor, the first step to developing a strength training program is to decide what type of exercise you would like to do. There are many different types of strength training exercises, such as weight lifting, bodyweight exercises, and calisthenics. It's important to choose exercises that you enjoy, as this will help you stick to the program and progress quickly.

The next step is to create a schedule for your program. It's important to give your body time to rest and recover between workouts, so be sure to plan your workouts accordingly.

You can also incorporate other activities, such as stretching and yoga, into your program to help improve flexibility and mobility.

It's also important to track your progress. When you first start a strength training program, begin with light weights and low repetitions. As you progress, gradually increase the weight and number of repetitions. Keeping track of your progress will help you stay motivated and reach your goals.

Finally, make sure to stay hydrated and fuel your body with proper nutrition. Eating a balanced diet will help you build muscle and stay healthy.

Developing a strength training program can be a great way to improve your physical fitness and overall health. With the right training, nutrition, and recovery, you can reach your goals and have fun doing it!

Developing a strength training program is important to reach your fitness goals and stay healthy. Consult with your doctor to ensure that you are healthy enough for exercise, and then decide which type of exercise you would like to do.

Create a schedule for your program, track your progress, and stay hydrated and fueled with proper nutrition. With the right program, you can have fun and reach your goals!

Developing a strength training program can be tracked by keeping a log of the workouts, and logging the amount of weight lifted, the number of reps completed, and rest periods. This helps to track progress and to adjust the program as needed. Additionally, strength training should be accompanied by proper hydration and nutrition to ensure the body is getting the proper nutrients for muscle growth and recovery.

Finally, it’s important to make sure you are working out safely and not pushing yourself too hard. Listen to your body and be aware of any pain or uneasiness. If something doesn’t feel right, take a break and adjust your program.

# Chapter 4

# Building Conditioning Through Cardiovascular Workouts

Cardiovascular workouts are a great way to build conditioning in your body. Cardiovascular exercise is any type of exercise that increases your heart rate and gets your blood pumping. Examples of cardiovascular exercise include running, jogging, biking, swimming, and walking. These types of exercises can help you to increase your endurance and build your aerobic capacity, which will help you to stay healthier and improve your overall fitness level.

By increasing your endurance, you will be able to perform activities for longer periods without feeling fatigued. Additionally, cardiovascular exercise can help to improve your cardiovascular health by reducing your risk for heart disease, stroke, and other health conditions. Regular cardiovascular exercise can also help to improve your breathing, as well as your overall energy levels.

In addition to improving your overall health, cardiovascular workouts can also help to build conditioning in your body. Regular cardiovascular exercise can help to increase your muscle strength and build your muscle mass. It can also help to improve your muscle coordination and flexibility, as well as your balance and agility. All of these benefits can help to make you more physically fit and better able to perform physical activities.

Finally, regular cardiovascular exercise can help to reduce your stress levels and improve your mental health. Exercise can help to reduce feelings of anxiety, depression, and fatigue, as well as improve your overall mood.

Overall, regular cardiovascular exercise can help to improve your overall health and build conditioning in your body. It can help to increase your endurance, muscle strength, and coordination, as well as reduce your stress levels and improve your mental health. So, if you're looking to become more physically fit, consider incorporating cardiovascular exercise into your weekly routine.

# 7 Importance of Cardiovascular workouts

**1. Improved Metabolism** - Cardiovascular workouts can help to improve your body's metabolism by increasing the number of calories your body burns. This can help to speed up your weight loss efforts and help you to reach your health and fitness goals.

**2. Increased Endurance** - Regular cardiovascular exercise can help to increase your endurance and aerobic capacity. This can help you to perform activities for longer periods without feeling fatigued.

**3. Improved Heart Health** - Cardiovascular workouts can help to improve your cardiovascular health by reducing your risk for heart disease, stroke, and other health conditions.

**4. Muscle Strength and Mass** - Regular cardiovascular exercise can help to increase your muscle strength and build your muscle mass. It can also help to improve your muscle coordination and flexibility, as well as your balance and agility.

**5. Stress Relief** - Exercise can help to reduce feelings of anxiety, depression, and fatigue, as well as improve your overall mood. This can help to reduce your stress levels and help you to feel more relaxed and energized.

**6. Improved Mental Health** - Regular exercise can help to improve your mental health by helping to improve your focus and concentration. It can also help to boost your self-confidence and reduce feelings of anxiety and depression.

**7. Weight Control** - Cardiovascular exercise can help to burn calories and regulate your appetite, which can help to manage your weight.

# Chapter 5

## Interval Training and Fartlek Workouts

Interval training and fartlek workouts are two popular forms of exercise that are used to increase aerobic and anaerobic capacity. Interval training is a type of high-intensity exercise that involves alternating periods of intense effort with periods of rest. The intensity of the effort is typically at or near the maximum level the individual can sustain for a short time. Fartlek workouts are similar to interval training but are more unstructured and involve varying the intensity and duration of the effort.

Interval training is an effective way to increase aerobic and anaerobic capacity, as well as overall fitness. It can also be used to improve speed and agility. Intervals are typically done in a controlled environment, such as a track or treadmill, where the intensity and duration of the intervals can be easily monitored. Interval training can be done with different types of exercises, such as running, cycling, rowing, and swimming.

Fartlek workouts are a less structured form of exercise that involves varying the intensity and duration of the effort. Fartlek workouts can be done on any terrain or surface, such as trails, hills, or roads. Fartlek workouts can be customized to the individual's fitness level and goals. They are a great way to mix up a workout and add variety to a training program.

Both interval training and fartlek workouts are excellent forms of exercise that can be used to increase aerobic and anaerobic capacity and overall fitness. They can be done on any terrain or surface and can be customized to the individual's fitness level and goals.

Whether you're looking to increase your aerobic and anaerobic capacity or just mix up your workout routine, interval training and fartlek workouts are great options.

These two types of exercise can help you reach your fitness goals, improve your speed and agility, and add variety to your routine.

If you're looking for a way to increase your fitness level, interval training and fartlek workouts are great ways to do it.

Interval training and fartlek workouts can help you reach your fitness goals and take your Workouts to the next level.

So, if you're looking for a way to mix up your Workouts and take your fitness to the next level, interval training, and fartlek workouts are great options.

Try them out and see how they can help you reach your fitness goals.

# Chapter 6

# Plyometric Training

Plyometric Training is an exercise technique used to increase muscular power and explosiveness. It involves a combination of jumping, hopping, and bounding movements that are designed to increase the speed of muscle contractions. Plyometric exercises can be used to increase speed, agility, and overall athletic performance. Plyometric training is often used in sports such as basketball, football, and track and field.

The goal of plyometric training is to increase the speed and power of muscle contractions by using a combination of dynamic jumps and bounds. Plyometric exercises involve high-intensity, explosive movements that use the body's momentum to create power and speed. To maximize the benefits of plyometric training, exercises should be performed with maximal effort and with proper form. Plyometric exercises should be performed in a controlled setting with a qualified coach or trainer.

Plyometric training can be beneficial for athletes of all levels and abilities. It can help to improve balance, coordination, agility, and power. Plyometric training can also help to increase the speed of muscle contraction, which can help athletes to perform better in their chosen sport. Additionally, plyometric exercises can help to improve joint stability, reduce the risk of injury, and improve muscular endurance.

Due to the high-intensity nature of plyometric training, it should be used in moderation and with caution. Beginners should start with low-intensity exercises and gradually increase intensity as their strength and coordination improves. It is important to work with a qualified coach or trainer to ensure that exercises are performed correctly and in the proper form.

Overall, plyometric training can be an effective way to improve athletic performance and reduce the risk of injury. It is important to use proper form and work with a qualified coach or trainer to ensure that exercises are performed safely and effectively.

By incorporating plyometric exercises into a regular workout routine, athletes can improve their speed and power, reduce their risk of injury, and increase their overall performance.

## 7 Importance of Plyometric Training

**1. Improve Speed:** Plyometric exercises are a great way to improve speed and agility. By performing exercises such as box jumps, squat jumps, and tuck jumps, athletes can increase the speed of their muscle contractions, allowing them to move more quickly.

**2. Increase Power:** Plyometric exercises are designed to increase muscular power and explosiveness. By performing exercises such as depth jumps and single-leg hops, athletes can increase their power output, which can help them perform better in their sport.

**3. Improve Balance and Coordination:** Plyometric exercises require the use of balance and coordination. By performing exercises such as lateral bounds and skater hops, athletes can improve their balance and coordination, which can help them perform better in their sport.

**4. Reduce Injury Risk:** Plyometric exercises can help to reduce the risk of injury by strengthening the muscles and joints. By performing exercises such as lateral jumps and bounding jumps, athletes can strengthen their muscles and joints, reducing their risk of injury.

**5. Increase Muscular Endurance:** Plyometric exercises can help to increase muscular endurance. By performing exercises such as lateral bounds and single-leg hops, athletes can increase their muscular endurance, allowing them to perform for longer

**6. Improve Joint Stability:** Plyometric exercises can help to improve joint stability. By performing exercises such as depth jumps and bounding jumps, athletes can strengthen their joints, allowing them to perform better in their sport.

**7. Increase Overall Athletic Performance:** Plyometric exercises can help to increase overall athletic performance. By performing exercises such as depth jumps and single-leg hops, athletes can increase their power and speed, allowing them to perform better in their sport.

Overall, plyometric training can be an effective way to improve athletic performance and reduce the risk of injury. It is important to use proper form and work with a qualified coach or trainer to ensure that exercises are performed safely and effectively. By incorporating plyometric exercises into a regular workout routine, athletes can improve their speed and power, reduce their risk of injury, and increase their overall performance.

# Chapter 7

# Principles of Recovery

**1. Self-Direction:** This principle emphasizes the importance of the individual being in control of their recovery journey, setting their own goals, and having autonomy in the decision-making process. This means that the individual is encouraged to make their own choices about what works best for them, with the necessary support from a network of professionals and peers.

**2. Individualized and Person-Centered:** This principle recognizes that every individual has different needs and that the recovery process should be tailored to their specific situation and goals. This means that the individual should be actively involved in the design of their treatment plan and should be supported in finding the right mix of services and interventions that will best support them in their recovery.

**3. Empowerment:** This principle emphasizes the importance of providing individuals in recovery with the necessary tools and resources to become self-sufficient and empowered. This includes ensuring that individuals have access to the necessary education, training, and employment opportunities, as well as other sources of social, emotional, and spiritual support.

**4. Holistic:** This principle recognizes that individuals in recovery must address all aspects of their lives, including physical, mental, emotional, and spiritual. This means that the individual should be supported in finding the right mix of services and interventions that will help them to address all aspects of their lives and foster overall health and well-being.

**5. Non-Linear:** This principle acknowledges that recovery is an ongoing process that does not follow a straight line. This means that individuals should be supported in understanding and navigating the ups and downs of the recovery journey, and should be encouraged to celebrate their successes and progress along the way.

**6. Strengths-Based:** This principle recognizes that individuals in recovery have unique strengths and capacities that should be identified, developed, and utilized to support their recovery. This means that individuals should be supported in identifying and leveraging their strengths and resources, as well as the strengths and resources of those in their support network.

**7. Peer Support:** This principle emphasizes the importance of providing individuals in recovery with a network of peers who can provide mutual understanding, support, guidance, and camaraderie. This means that individuals should be encouraged to establish and maintain meaningful relationships with other individuals in recovery, as well as other peers who can offer hope and encouragement.

**8. Hope:** This principle recognizes the importance of maintaining and nurturing hope throughout the recovery process. This means that individuals should be encouraged to believe in themselves and their ability to achieve a meaningful and satisfying life, despite the challenges that they may face.

**9. Respect:** This principle emphasizes the importance of treating individuals in recovery with respect, dignity, and understanding. This means that individuals should be treated with respect in all aspects of their recovery journey, and should be supported in finding the right mix of services and interventions that will best meet their needs.

**10. Responsibility:** This principle emphasizes the importance of individuals taking responsibility for their recovery and for their role in supporting the recovery of others. This means that individuals should be supported in developing the necessary skills and resources for achieving and maintaining their recovery, as well as for supporting the recovery of others.

These principles of recovery can provide individuals and their support networks with a framework for understanding and navigating the recovery process. It is important to remember that recovery is an ongoing process and that individuals will face many challenges and setbacks along the way.

By focusing on these principles and utilizing the necessary resources, individuals can work towards achieving and maintaining a meaningful and satisfying life in recovery.

# Chapter 8

## Common Injuries and How to Avoid Them

Injuries are an extremely common occurrence in everyday life. Whether it's from playing sports, participating in activities, or just everyday life, there is always a risk of injury. Some injuries we can't avoid, but there are several ways to minimize our risk of getting injured.

Here are some common injuries and how to avoid them.

**Sprains and strains:** Sprains and strains are two of the most common injuries, and they are usually caused by overuse or overexertion of a muscle or joint. To avoid sprains and strains, you should always warm up and stretch before any physical activity, and make sure to cool down and stretch afterward. You should also be mindful of your form and technique when lifting or exercising.

**Fractures:** Fractures happen when a bone is broken, and they can happen due to falls, trauma, or overuse. To prevent fractures, you should be sure to wear protective gear when participating in sports or activities. You should also be aware of your environment and be sure to watch where you're walking or running.

**Concussions:** Concussions are caused by a blow to the head, and they can be caused by a fall, contact sports, or an auto accident. To avoid concussions, you should always wear proper protective gear when playing contact sports, and be sure to buckle up when in a vehicle.

**Lacerations:** Lacerations are cuts and scrapes that can be caused by anything from falls to contact sports. To avoid lacerations, you should always be aware of your environment and watch where you're walking. You should also wear appropriate protective gear when playing contact sports.

**Dislocations:** Dislocations occur when a joint becomes displaced from its normal position. To prevent dislocations, you should always warm up and stretch before any physical activity, and never overexert your joints.

Injuries can be unavoidable, but there are several steps we can take to minimize our risk of getting injured. It's important to always stretch, warm up, and wear appropriate protective gear when participating in physical activities.

By following these steps, we can significantly reduce our risk of injury.

The best way to avoid injury is to stay aware of your body and environment and to always take the necessary precautions. If you feel any pain or discomfort, it's best to take a break and rest. By following these steps, we can ensure that we stay healthy and safe.

No one likes to get injured, but it's important to understand the risks and take the necessary steps to prevent them. By following the steps outlined above, we can reduce our risk of common injuries and stay safe.

Being proactive in taking steps to avoid injury can help us stay healthy and active, and enjoy the activities we love without worry.

So, the next time you're participating in physical activity, keep these tips in mind to ensure you stay safe and injury-free.

# Conclusion

Unlocking the secrets of athletic performance is a journey that can take a lifetime to master. Through strength and conditioning, athletes can develop their physical capabilities to the highest levels. It takes dedication and hard work to get there, but the rewards are great. Strength and conditioning can help improve speed, power, agility, and endurance; all of which are essential components of athletic performance. With the right guidance, athletes can unlock the secrets of athletic performance and become the best they can be. With the right training program in place, athletes can be sure that they are maximizing their potential and taking their performance to the next level.

In conclusion, unlocking the secrets of athletic performance is an ongoing process that requires dedication, hard work, and the right guidance. By understanding the importance of strength and conditioning, athletes can unlock the secrets of athletic performance and become the best they can be. With a well-structured training program, athletes can maximize their potential and take their performance to the next level.

All of this can be achieved over time, with the right approach and support from coaches and trainers. Unlocking the secrets of athletic performance is a journey that can take a lifetime to master, but the rewards are great.

With knowledge and understanding, athletes can unlock the secrets of athletic performance and take their performance to the next level. By taking the time to learn about strength and conditioning, athletes can become the best version of themselves and unlock the secrets of athletic performance.

www.ingramcontent.com/pod-product-compliance
Lightning Source LLC
LaVergne TN
LVHW020534160826
845677LV00015B/4061
* 9 7 9 8 3 7 4 5 1 6 3 4 0 *